Ava L. Reis

Dreams that drowned in purple Whisky

AF237509

Ava L. Reis

Dreams that drowned in purple Whisky

a collection of poems

1.   Edition August 2021

Bibliographic information on the German National Library:

The German National Library lists this publication in the German National Bibliography; detailed bibliographic data is available on the Internet at http://dnb.dnb.de.

Manufacturing and publishing: BoD – Books on Demand, Norderstedt

ISBN: 978-3-7543-3718-9

Dedicated to all the miserable souls who wonder if I'm writing about their cruelties.

I truly am.

Foreword

Poetry isn't born with the intention of one specific meaning, it
rather gets it through being interpreted.
It is a form of storytelling, that gives readers a chance to put
their own thoughts and feelings into it.
Just like music, but the beat is your own pace while reading.

Please feel free to give my work a meaning.

I. IMMORTAL'S DEATH

From the ashes the eagle spreads his wings.
The very last riddle to be solved,
the riddle of the sphinx.
Mists of centuries, it had evolved.

Mysterious creature bathing in darkness,
while the cage was filled with a guiding light.
Out of the cage there sparkles,
the riddles solving knight.

Teardrops of ice on his arm.
The sphinx reared up in front of him.
Reared up and growled »He will do harm,
he who is the king.

Has never been born,
and will never die.
Tell me without your words being torn,
who is he? I don't accept a lie.«

But the knight didn't fear the threat.
He was there to die, not to pass the test.
Shouted the words, shook his head,
and put his hand up to his chest.

»Surrender will have us released.
Yes, I believe the flowers will bloom,
the man you're looking for, is the sun in the east,
the grave has been built, who's to be entombed?«

II.   THE DROUGHT

River, river wild and blue,
I'll be the only one for you.
Take me to your stormy grave,
past the ruins of your shapeless wave.

River, river cruel and cold,
you took away my golden blood,
my strength, my warmth, my soul.
Made me yours in eternity, we are whole.

Oh River, river softened stones,
share with me your silver throne.
There will never be more sorrow,
than when I'll just be drowning, tomorrow.

River, river take my bones,
wash my sins to make me yours.
Lost my love inside your arms,
please, let me be within your charms.

Lovely River, River dead heartbeat,
murdered quick the peaceful fleet.
Stole the radiance of my daydream,
desperately trying to warm your cold bloodstream.

Yet River, river, wild and blue,
I owe my love to only you.

III.   THE FLOOD

Sand, oh sand spreading roughly across the land,
cutting off the river's wedding band.
Sorrows underneath, crushing forcibly into the seas,
our pleadings we quietly reprise.

Sand my dear, your love has spoken,
we can't listen to it, even if we are widely woken.
Scream at us, or speak in silence,
desperately pleading not to leave us in this violence.

Lying in your graceful arm,
pretending to do me no harm.
Just a quiet memory,
beautiful times carried away by history.

You pushed us away from your precious self,
like the wind blowing the photos off the shelf.
If only you would know,
how all those cities lost their glow.

Now you're gone with all your glimmer,
nothing left, not even a slight shimmer.
Come back and make us one,
with or without you, our souls are lost and gone.

IV.   THE VIRUS

Sometimes I can't believe,
how unable we are to grieve.
Plastic in the ocean,
we are blind for all emotion.

No matter where you look,
watch the news or read a book.
Hunting for joy, but not to solve hunger,
would you've thought about that, when you were younger?

Animals going extinct.
Why can't we realize, that we all are linked?
To those beautiful species and varieties.
Instead, we raise our children with anxieties.

So much suffering and tears, still we close our eyes.
Demanding change, but not seeing the lies.
Stories made up, solely to distract from what matters,
be honest, our world is in tatters.

Air pollution and factories not willing to care,
don't tell me you can't see the dust in the air.
And people pretending, that one can't make a change,
without noticing this is cruel and unhealthily strange.

History has proven that a single soul can transform,
I guess it's time to finally brainstorm,
how to save our planet and our solar system.
Aren't we humans the species with the greatest wisdom?

And yet, we not only destroy our home, but that of others.
Even though, most of us don't try to be bothered.
Burning trees and rising seas,
you can call it what you want, but mankind is the disease.

V.   ART OF TONE

If only you could see what I see,
your eyes are the definition of being free.
The grace on your lips as you peacefully smile,
your music gives people wings to fly, at least for a while.

You are the simple expression of admiration,
perceiving life in ecstatic elation.
Melting and becoming one with your dreams,
not naked but covered in skinny jeans.

My darling, you are the most beautiful picture,
or the most stunning sculpture.
Nothing heals more than the fervor of your art,
never tear your gift apart.

You see things others don't,
you feel the music where others won't.
Sound, my torch, you bring love to places so empty,
that couldn't be filled by a thousand hearts, or brandy.

The twinkle that guides you, is hope's shine.
Express your feelings, don't drown them in wine.
My love, my flower you brought my life some change,
that I will never rearrange.

VI. I SEE THE MOUNTAINS MOVING

All those witty, wise and generous minds,
gathered in the room no one easily finds,
to discuss on how to handle tragedy.
Or maybe, to guide through all this mystery.

The fact that they can't see the problem,
nor find a way to solve their boredom,
doesn't bother them any more, than cold coffee does.
One of them is always stroking his miserable fuzz.

»I see the mountains moving!«,
Screamed the apprentice without them approving.
»Look out the window and insure yourself,
I fear the motions of the continental shelf!«.

Young fellow was terrified by what he had witnessed,
seeing stones colliding, the smallest with the biggest.
The peaceful landscape that was there before,
is now gone, for evermore.

»Stop telling lies young man! « one of the elder grunted,
making the apprentice one of the most wanted.
He wouldn't dare to risk a blink,
knowing if he was wrong, his arrogance could shrink.

»Please, oh, please forget my young age,
we are all in danger, sitting in this cage!«.
The apprentice tried to get the men out of the room,
but they insisted staying inside, not willing to accept their
doom.

Hoping to get back to his family tonight,
the young man started pulling on the elderly, holding them
tight.
He couldn't get them to leave the house,
on his mind the baby boy, held by his spouse.

How perfectly his wife's hair smelled,
and how soft her skin felt,
he thought, while the building started trembling over.
Ashes and bricks willing to cover.

Sometimes ignorance is bliss,
but the young man is the one we will miss.
Trying to save those lives, who don't want to be salvaged.
The great building burying him, is now ravaged.

Next to him are all the elder men,
being wrong once again.
Moving mountains had no place in none of their minds,
they killed a brave man, now there's just a memorial that
reminds.

VII. WHEN THE VULTURE EATS
THE CULTURE

Two lost souls devour what nature has left.
Savannah took the breath of life.
Empty bones the drought did cleft,
out of the bones vulture will thrive.

Nothing there to give them shelter,
glistening sun that evaporates water.
In the bare beauty of the delta,
days ago, unity did slaughter.

Picking the pieces apart,
of what once was a beautiful gazelle,
with a beating heart.
Empty cries for a farewell.

Dead meat begging to be treated mean.
Vulture covered in rotten blood,
wrapped in red, like a queen.
Poured sap of life over the flower bud.

Singing the song of devastation across the land.
Though the vulture didn´t bother to kill,
he´s the one deleting the tracks in the sand,
with nothing else, but his pure will.

One day the rain will come.
Drops on the ground.
All the suffering and blood will be gone,
and nature will be dancing to the majestic sound.

VIII.   THE VOID

Dolphins in the bush,
camels in the sea.
The cliff ends with a push,
innocently sailing downwards, so feathery.

New world order.
Peaceful darkness, flooded with artificial light,
like an incurable disorder.
Empty messages we still recite.

Wondering if I am going insane,
taking one last sip,
viscous poison running through every vein,
experiencing rearrangement's very drip.

Reliability is banned,
lighthouse built under the surface.
Can't drown with your head under the Sand.
Our tidings floating shallow and wordless.

Incubating the fire with the need to keep it alive.
Suffocating it with barbecue sauce,
making everything better as we strive,
inexorably creates loss.

Fear of protecting what we have with our wages,
leads to new inventions.
Dismantling what had worked for ages,
secret, that nobody mentions.

The need to write something positive,
or the need to spread the joy,
makes me unable to breath.
Don't worry it's all just a ploy.

IX.   FOOLING SUNLIGHT

I have never been a person, able to express how I'm feeling,
my inside can't be very revealing,
though I would like to explain how much you mean to me.
So, I will tell you in a verse or three.

You bring me joy you bring me laughter,
by a joke or trying to be a drafter.
I want to be happy, yet my obsessive-compulsive disorder,
beats me like a broken recorder.

What would I give, to laugh like you can,
while sitting in the back of a broken van.
I wish I could take life with ease.
No misgivings, if you worry, you just cease.

You don't decide on the road,
but to leave behind that heavy load.
Plenty of time to rest in your grave,
for now, escape the duty's tidal wave.

X. FOR THE MOON

Wherever you might want to go,
remember, that time will flow.
What we sow, we reap,
yet don't forget: some are wolves, disguised as sheep.

Never feel guilty of what is not your fault,
because that is a wound, treated with salt.
Stop obscuring your senses with this poison,
it will narrow your extremely wide horizon.

My moon, the closer you are, the more I am afraid,
afraid of losing you, afraid that your light would fade.
I never understood how precious you are,
in fact, you are more than just a dimly lit star.

Be happy and recognize the sun as your power,
don't build a wall, or entrench yourself in a tower.
Show the world who the moon really is,
you are the kindness, that the world shouldn't miss.

You control the tides.
If you can't decide, I'd love to be the one that guides.
Stronger than you could ever dream of,
defeating your enemies with nothing, but pure love.

My moon you are so far away, yet so close.
Never apart, neither through day nor the distance we chose.
Lovely moon, if you ever feel sad, flustered or raged,
remember: I'm only one call away.

XI. YOU FOUND THE LOST MAN

While he was lying on her chest, pretending to sleep,
but listening to her heartbeat,
his little brother came up to the resting couple,
sitting down, watching them cuddle.

»I am so glad he met you« begins the little brother to speak his
kind words,
»Without you, he was irritated and loud, trying to hide form all
that hurts.
But now he is a good man,
even listening, if he can.

And I promise, he'll take care of his greatest treasure,
with nothing else, but the greatest pleasure.
You calmed him down, and showed him some manners,
now, everybody can see the great man behind the canvas.«

Little brother smiled proudly,
but for her, the sunny day was suddenly cloudy.
»That sounds horrible« she said, as tears ran down her face,
»It sounds like I'm an awful woman, taking away his grace.

I didn't mean to tame a wild mind,
bounding him by his bones and them to grind.
He is meant to be free, even by my side.
Never wanted his character to hide.«

Little brother tried to explain why she wasn´t right,
but before he could answer, the man held her tight.
»Darling you calmed a devastating storm,
not only devastating him, but his family and his home.

Without you, I wouldn't be living,
I would be nothing without your love, constantly giving.
You are my salvation, you found me when I was lost,
for you I would sell my life, no matter the cost.«

XII.   ANGELA

Stay wild earth child,
tender mist but still so wild.
Can't dim the glare of your inner glow.
It shines so bright, so let it show.

Pack your bags, forget the chores,
there's no freedom behind closed doors.
Remember the good times, but never look back,
be who you are, yet stay on track.

The road will guide you to a place,
of such incomprehensible grace.
Your body will find the time to rest,
my child, you are so blessed.

Open your eyes, oh don't they show,
your minds vehicle, drifting through the afterglow.
Bathe in sunshine, let it be your kindling,
your journey – iron and carbon are mingling.

XIII.   THE TROUSERS WERE TOO TIGHT

She loved the look,
she loved the pattern of flowers,
using it to cook,
or even to shower.

Never would she take them off,
not realizing, that her feet were slowly dying.
Couldn't even risk to cough,
yet changing would leave her crying.

The toes were blue and swollen,
no more control of her muscles.
Only way to move is crawling,
finally, she found the last piece of her jigsaw puzzles.

The image there made it clear,
the trousers were too tight,
the words she never wanted to hear:
If she can't take them off, they'll kill her tonight.

XIV. THE CAKE WAS ROTTEN
BEFORE BAKING

Is there a reason to start something that's already dead?
Was the question, that came up in my head.
The batter was moldy,
even though you claimed it was holy.

Stirring the dried dough,
while watching your awful show.
Seeing you perform that piece of madness,
filling my vivacity with sadness.

Chocolate so old it turned grey,
you told me to move on, what a cliché.
Of course, the grass is greener when it's fake,
still, I am standing there to bake.

Sometimes it's better to remove what is rotten,
because you waste the new life, you could have gotten.
But something makes me hold onto what hurts,
obviously making everything worse.

Putting the moldy dough with the grey chocolate in the oven,
caught in a circle, created by a simple coven.
Trying to save the memories of a good cake,
the ones not moldy before attempting to bake.

Realizing that the cake will be hard as a stone,
maybe I'll be fine, as soon as you leave me alone.
Your heart is as cold as ice,
throw away what is dead, is the best advice.

Our cake was rotten before baking.
Oh, how my poor wits are aching.
Your favorite ingredient is misery,
I guess the moldy, grey and rotten times are history.

XV.   ANNE BONNY

Oh Anne,
never happy with a man.
Your sword sparkles in the night,
wouldn't you have loved to be a knight?

Fighting braver than a man,
even if you say »that's all I can«.
I know you are so much more,
than Rackham's lady off the shore.

Your unbreakable passion for the ocean,
isn't enough to cover the wounds of emotion.
Childhood spent in men's clothes,
as an adult, it was their freedom that you chose.

Seeing Mary die,
weren't you tired of being the bad guy?
Fleeing from that deadly cell,
into your and your father's hell.

Oh Anne, wouldn't you have loved to be a mother?
For your son and his little baby brother.
Jumped off the boat to say goodbye,
I bet you didn't even dare to cry.

Anne, my dear Anne,
if you met a good man,
you wouldn't have become that pirate legend I adore,
and many women would still live frightened to the core.

Dear Anne, I wish you a good rest,
though your heart is torn apart off your chest.
The sea will watch and wait,
until you are free, leaving the last gate.

XVI.   THE LOST HAT

It was all she ever wanted,
all she ever was.
Her way to identify,
glancing up at the sky.

A short moment of imprudence,
being followed by a group of students.
Like losing a bet,
but to the devil, she has recently met.

She said, there is no reason to cry,
I just need a new hat to buy.
Clearly, she can't see,
the sentiments are to disagree.

In the end, there is nothing left,
solely an empty shelf, abandoned by the theft.
All is lost, she is no more free,
only, because the bloody hat is now resting on a tree.

XVII. THE WITCH WHO COULDN'T CONJURE

Spell bottles and candy jars,
cards all over the table.
Always giving hate towards protein bars,
never allowed to enter the neighbor's stable.

It's said she rides through the night on a golden broom,
but lately she had to make adjustments in transportation.
When it broke in half, like a fake silver spoon,
since that moment, she misses the power spell's creation.

Candles burning night and day,
yet nothing worked for her.
She couldn't stand to betray,
not even burning an ounce of myrrh.

What is a witch without magic?
Her hand of golden rings was bloody.
Nothing, and sheer tragic.
With a dead sheep she ended her nature study.

»Why don't your spells work?«
her clients asked all the time.
Forming her lips into a smirk,
she promised, »They'll be fine«.

»Maybe it's the alcohol that steals my witchcraft«,
said the witch and opened up another bottle of wine.
»I am just so understaffed,
don't get mad and count to nine!«

Client began to count, starting by one,
quiet at first but then got louder.
While the witch rambled about the midnight sun,
facing client who believed, and also the doubter.

Two, three and four,
mixing a potion, fixing the kettle with bricks.
The numbers went by as she began to pour.
Tasted on five and stopped pouring at six.

Meeting number seven,
people felt deceived.
Witch greeted people in heaven,
leaving them endlessly peeved.

When the counting hit the eight,
slowly breathing in,
she smiled and said »checkmate«.
Gracefully lift her chin.

By the time the nine was spoken,
on the table appeared a black swan.
The silence in the crowd was broken,
there was nothing left, the witch was gone.

XVIII.   LOSING WEIGHT BY GAINING IT

Everything that is mass-produced loses its worth,
bigger and bigger becomes the girth.
But we are getting sicker,
with every piece about which we bicker.

There once were plenty of fish in the sea,
now there is plenty of hungry people, needing to flee.
Why are we closing our eyes to reality?
With every year we grow, we lose three.

Running out of time, but not everyone wants to notice,
like trying to break a wall with a stick, simply hopeless.
The cradle of devastation rocks happily,
while we are moving like robots, absently.

More and more is wanted, but nothing is needed,
the flowers for our grave have already been seeded.
Take a step back and enjoy the trip,
not long until humanity loses the road's grip.

Only thing we don't have, but desire is love,
like the wings to fly, needed by a dove.
Love more and waste less,
nobody deserves to live in this mess.

XIX. GUITAR WITH BROKEN STRINGS

Zest is astray,
strangled dreams on the scale of horizon aweigh.
Do I find peace, or do I have to forget,
about all the things I should regret?

I think back to when we went out in late September,
hoping it's the carefree times, we'll remember.
When you sat there in the park, I have to admit,
the gleaming fell in love with the unlit.

Playing your beautiful song,
never hitting a single note wrong.
I should have captured this feeling,
it was the only thing leading to healing.

Your voice went up and down,
the moonlight falling on your head, like a crown.
Making you the Witcher that you are,
able to capture a single star.

I miss those times, but now you are broken,
not a single tone to be spoken.
Your strings are loose,
wood splinters, the remains of your body, nothing left to use.

XX. ADDICTION

I wish you all the best,
finally, let me have some rest.
Swimming in the ocean,
lying there without any motion.

By stealing all my energy,
you made sure I'm chained, and never free.
Wasn't it the contract of love that you signed?
Begging you to keep the details in mind.

Be committed, don't go away,
neither to the mountains nor to a stormy bay.
Yet, you took my life and possessions,
you are the tale of fake love's confessions.

What is taking without giving?
Just your way to make a living.
Stole my money and my cars,
you'd be safer behind bars.

I guess this is the lesson to learn,
some things in life you've got to earn.
And others you simply deserve,
even if they are killing your last nerve.

XXI.   THE SPILLED LAVENDER
TEA

Purple dots on the table,
dripping on the cable.
The abandoned cup standing next to it,
watching all of it, every single bit.

Broken pieces of her brothers,
and some of many others,
dying on the floor.
Fragments which can't be whole, nevermore.

Was it a fight?
Or maybe just a result of a night?
A night filled with so much alcohol,
that the beautiful cups were thrown into a wall.

He called her the daughter of witches,
probably deserved the seven stitches.
All that because of simple lavender tea,
that she planned to spill into a tree.

XXII.   OWNERSHIP OF HURT

Blame it all on my existence.
Told me about how you will treat me better.
My defense? Passive resistance.
Hopes or Dead dreams? I guess the latter.

Hiding my eyes from things I need to notice.
You are my downfall,
simply hopeless,
yet still my port of call.

Promised me, you wouldn't do it again.
You love me, I am the wood your fiery soul is needing.
More than I think you are, so tell me then:
Why are my lips still bleeding?

Won´t let me leave,
clasps my arm like a vice,
don't bother to deceive.
Storm disasters above our paradise.

I am your possession.
Unable to breathe,
without your confession.
Inside my core, the blood does already seethe.

You are my addiction,
breaking me inside and out.
Oh, empathic intelligence, help me with eviction,
give me shelter, somewhere to hideout.

Abuse me, love me, hate me,
hold me tight then throw me into the ditch.
I am your firewood that once was a tree,
I am what holds your cold heart warm. The bleeding wound´s
stitch.

XXIII.   ANGEL FALLING IN LOVE WITH BEING EVIL

The night is bright and so is the day,
all is likely to betray.
Heated darkness floating over the cold side of the sun,
when the tragedy of romance begun.

Dying starts when you are born,
sacrificing noise blown through a silver horn.
Feelings bursting to the sound,
floating souls of those, who touched the forbidden lake and
drowned.

Shadow sitting silently on a cloud,
screaming his silence out so loud.
Angel once good, now evil,
falling so tremendously for a power called the devil.

The pure heart traded for deadly love,
still sitting on the cloud, watching from above.
When the darkness hits the light,
there will neither be day, nor night.

There is a power stronger than the tides,
whatever you try, there is nothing that divides.
But bare in mind, there will come a time of fog so grey,
you'll hear the bell out of the grave, so devil's sins are washed
away.

XXIV. THE INTELLIGENCE OF LOVE

It was only, when she fell in love with the man,
who looked like the spitting image of herself,
realizing, she adored her looks more than she thought she can,
suddenly venerating every angle of the photos on the shelf.

She started to laugh without a joke being told,
and to dance without music playing.
Those endless layers of mold,
in which her mind was covered in, she started slaying.

When she fell in love with the man, looking like her reflection,
bringing her so much joy and bliss,
she finally realized her own perfection,
with each and every kiss.

Love is an indescribable thing,
yet for her it was salvation.
A strange combination between the queen and her king.
He never tried to take away her emancipation.

Prejudice is what her friends chose,
judging how similar they looked.
»He looks like a girl, with his female clothes«.
Not capturing the feeling, of which they were hooked.

So she gazed into the eyes of her love,
finally detecting who she was.

Forgetting about the people, who were trying to shove.
Stereotypes became irrelevant, like earth took a pause.

Even though he wasn't as tall as her,
she finally was confident enough to wear heels.
See, how shallow opinions lose their spur.
Her self-confidence, in which he gently appeals.

Her friend claimed while pointing at his straw hat:
»He isn't really a man with his androgynous style!«
»He is everything and even more than that,
stop being so narrowminded and vile!

He is braver than every man I met.
Maybe with his style of dress you cannot agree,
protecting and guarding, I shall not forget.
Let me tell you, he is not afraid, to be me«

XXV.   BATHING IN BEER

Bathtub filled with beer,
human's eyes watching the distant peer.
Noble men walking down to the harbor,
none of them showing any ardor.

Still, the man was fascinated by their sight,
no expression of delight.
Yet they seemed to be bound by more than resentment.
United, but all independent.

Bathing in beer,
in the distance ships floating into the dimly lit pier.
Human grabs the bottle tighter,
trying not to lose his meaning, like a fighter.

Fisherman on the shore,
leaving the dry land of the night once more.
Singing in a choir,
about all of their hidden desire.

One more sip of that liquid gold,
his fate he so desperately tried to remold.
Sitting in his bathtub with a view of the pier,
enjoying hundred last sips of his beer.

As the fisherman's choir stops to sing,
it's the man and his voice tuning in.
Singing about the loss of his beloved Leigh-Anne,
truly she deserved a better man.

»Leigh-Anne, my true love, where have you gone?«,
sang the man in his sad song,
»You promised me you'd stay around,
now you're gone, and I am downed.

Leigh-Anne, my true love, why did you die,
we were not even on the peak, could have gotten so high.
You were more beautiful than anyone could describe,
inside and out, there was nothing to hide«.

While the man proceeded to sing his sad words,
the pier started burning because of the lords.
They were playing with fire,
underestimating it, climbing higher and higher.

Bright light,
melting the once unbreakable darkness of the night.
Lighting a way to another dimension,
the fire was free, there could be no tension.

The fisherman tried to save what has always been theirs,
while the peerage just stands there, immovable and stares.
All their attempts were in vain,
a desperate scream cut the nightly air with pain.

The first ship burned down to his skeleton, showing every
single bone,
the man couldn't see it, he heard no tone.
No tone reached his ears,
from the devastated voices that screamed from the piers.

Couldn't hear the ship breaking down,
or watching it sink, meeting the oceans ground.
He didn't listen to the fires meeting the seas,
rats leaving the ships and also their fleas.

Harbor burning light and bright,
you may ask, why all of that was out of his sight.
He didn't see none of that,
because his ears were covered in beer, under water was his head.

Finally, he heard something that broke his inner silence,
but it wasn't the fisherman screaming in violence,
it was the sound of his love's voice,
talking, begging and giving him one last choice.

For him there was no question to debate,
whether to come with her or not, it happened and he couldn't await.
And while the noble and the fisherman burned on the pier,
the lonely man was drowning in his bathtub of beer.

EPILOGUE

In this collection of poems, you can find two types of rhymes.

1. Rhyming couplet:
The last word of the first two lines rhyme and the last words of the third and fourth line rhyme.

A
A
B
B

2. Alternate rhyme:
The last word of the first line rhymes with the third and the last word of the second line rhymes with the fourth.

A
B
A
B

Each poem creates its own flow through the use of either one of those rhyming techniques. I don't use them consciously, they rather seem to fit one way or another.

The rhyming techniques are surely not the only things to consider. The flow of words also matters, and within that, the repeating of some words does as well. I think it is quite fascinating how you can rise tension by repeating words in general, or by repeating them at a certain point in the verse.

I'm well aware, that I still have a lot to learn, especially when it comes to writing poetry, but this collection was a genuine journey, and an absolute pleasure to write.
My personal goal is to distract people from whatever they may be going through right now, and maybe – if I'm lucky– give

them another perspective on how they see this astounding place we get to live in.

Some of my work might seem dark, or even sinister to you, but remember: Flowers wither when the sun is constantly evaporating their water. Eagle owls, as well as many other beautiful animals, are nocturnal. There is no day without the night, no calm without a storm, and especially no good without the bad. It's what makes us feel grateful for the sunshine, without taking it for granted.

If you want to join me on my journey of writing – stay tuned, I am working on the next collection.

Stay safe and be kind.

Love,

Ava